WoodenTeeth
& Jelly Beans
The Tupperman Files

Ray Nelson ★ Douglas Kelly ★ Ben Adams ★ Mike McLane

Scholastic Inc.

New York
Toronto
London
Auckland
Sydney

For Holly

ISBN 0-590-97439-4

Copyright © 1995 by Flying Rhinoceros, Inc.
All rights reserved. Published by Scholastic Inc., 555 Broadway, New York, NY 10012, by arrangement with Beyond Words Publishing, Inc.

12 11 10 9 8 7 6 5 4   6 7 8 9/9 0 1/0

Printed in the U.S.A.   09

First Scholastic printing, October 1996

I was once honored to be President of the United States of America. I had the privilege to sit in the same Oval Office and walk the same White House halls as Abraham Lincoln, Teddy Roosevelt, and John F. Kennedy. We all got there through persistence, hard work and, most importantly, education.

Within this book, you will learn about the lives of each president and what he faced while holding our nation's highest office. You will see that every president has at least one thing in common with you—each was a human being. They enjoyed hobbies, pets, and friends and worked at other jobs before becoming president. Not every student will become president, but everyone *can* become president.

For me, being President of the United States was both an honor and fun. This will be true for the dream you choose to pursue. Begin now by building your greatest asset—an education.

Gerald R. Ford

Gerald R. Ford

SOME WORDS YOU'LL NEED TO KNOW

Ambassador — A person appointed to represent his or her government in its relations with other governments.

Assassination — The murder of a famous person.

Cabinet — A group of people picked by the president to run different departments and to act as advisors.

Congress — The top law-making group in the United States. It consists of the Senate and the House of Representatives.

Constitution — The document that sets forth the system of basic laws and beliefs that guide the functions and the limits of the government in running the country.

Continental Congress — The group of individuals that ran the United States during the revolutionary times (1774 to 1789). This group was organized to voice concerns against Great Britain, to organize the Continental Army, and to serve as the executive and law-making arms of the government.

Declaration of Independence — The proclamation by the Continental Congress declaring the 13 American colonies politically independent from Great Britain.

Impeachment — To charge the president with wrongdoing in office before a proper court of justice. This is the first step in removing a president from office.
(See presidents John Tyler, Andrew Johnson, and Richard Nixon.)

Inauguration or inaugural — To enter into the office of president with a formal ceremony and/or celebration.

Secede — To formally withdraw from a membership or alliance.

Veto — The power under the Constitution that the president has to reject a bill that has been passed by Congress.

eaves began falling and the weather turned cool.
An election was brewing in Rhino Grade School.

The best and the brightest are running this year,
to lead Rhino School to the future frontier.
Whom will they choose? What will they do?
They'll all have to vote for one of these two.

TO THE "TOP"

★ WITH ★
TUPPERMAN

Tommy Tupperman is quiet and shy.
He's a little bit boring, he's just a bit dry.
(OK, here's the real truth.)
He has lifeless hair, his clothes are all blah.
His overall dullness will leave you in awe.
His face is real plain, he'll make you feel numb.
There's a whole lot more fun in an old wad of gum.
(But other than that, he's a really nice kid!)

Penelope Ratsworth is one of the two.
If she doesn't beat Tommy, she might beat on you.
She has a slight temper and sometimes she's rude.
She acts like a pit bull in a bad mood.
She's quick with a promise, she goes with the flow,
And if you don't vote for her, she'll step on your toe.

VOTE FOR

RATSWORTH

When the polls came out,
  Tommy said with a sigh,
  "I'm getting lambasted—why do I try ?

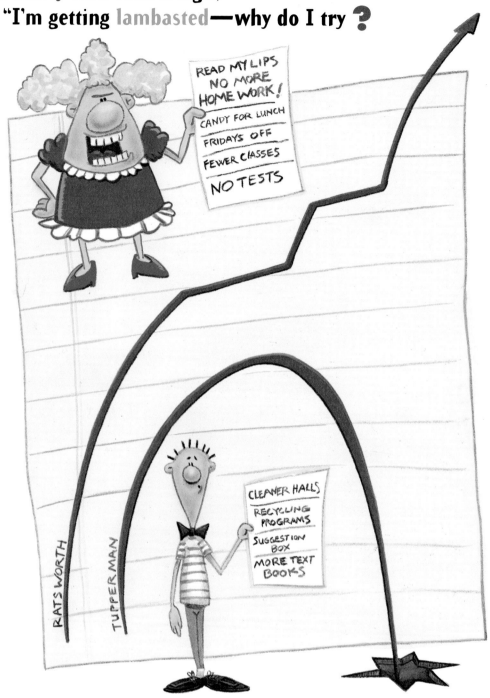

I stick by my morals,
 I try not to bend,
  but my rating is lower than an earthworm's rear end!

$\mathbb{P}$eople don't like me, not one little bit.
Maybe, just maybe, it's best if I quit."

Our hero **Tommy** was filled with despair,
When he came eye to eye with a powerful glare.
George looked at **Tommy**, and he seemed to say,

"I cannot
believe that
you're acting
this way!"

Tommy began feeling
a small bit of shame,
He realized that quitting
wasn't part of this game.

There's an election to win,
there's no time to rest.
We must get to work,
we can learn from the best.

THE TUPPERMAN FILES

PRESIDENTS

Born February 22, 1732 (Fredericksburg, Virginia)
Died December 14, 1799
Party No party (first term); Federalist (second term)
Vice president John Adams
Physical 6 feet 2 inches tall, 175 pounds
Family WIFE "Lady" Martha Custis SON John DAUGHTER Martha
[both adopted by Washington]

✪ PERSONAL ✪

Washington liked to play billiards and cards.
He also enjoyed reading newspapers and taking daily walks.

★
Fire!

George Washington loved to help fight fires.

★
Favorite Foods

Crabmeat soup and egg nog

★
What Happened?

1789 - First official Thanksgiving

1789 - First Postmaster General: Timothy Pickering

(The Postmaster General is in charge of running the U.S. postal system.)

1791 - Eli Whitney's cotton gin was invented (for refining harvested cotton)

1791 - First U.S. Mint (where money is made)

1791 - First U.S. Census (a count of all the people in an area)

★
I Have a Splinter in My Tongue—Not!

No! George Washington *did not* own a pair
of false teeth made out of wood. He did wear false teeth,
but his first pair were made of hippopotamus ivory.
He also had teeth made of lead, ivory,
and the teeth of humans, sheep, and cows.

★
Crossing the Delaware

As the commander of the Continental Army,
General Washington once led troops across
an iced-filled Delaware River to
win an important battle.

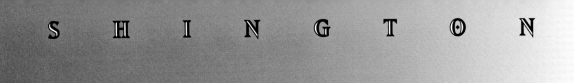
★
I Cannot Tell a Lie–I Lied

George Washington never said, "I cannot tell a lie, 'twas I cut down the cherry tree." This story, along with some other tall tales, came from a book written in 1800 called *The Life of George Washington; With Curious Anecdotes, Equally Honorable to Himself and Exemplary to His Young Countrymen.*

✪ PRESIDENTIAL FIRSTS ✪

First president to be younger than his wife

★

First to have his picture on a postage stamp

P R E S I D E N T

2

1797-1801

Born October 30, 1735 (Braintree [now Quincy], Massachusetts)
Died July 4, 1826 (the same day Thomas Jefferson died)
Party Federalist
Vice president Thomas Jefferson
Physical 5 feet 7 inches tall, 190 pounds
Family WIFE Abigail Smith   SONS John Quincy, Charles, and Thomas
DAUGHTER Abigail ("Nabby")

✪ PRESIDENTIAL FIRSTS ✪

First vice president elected to the presidency

★

First to live in the White House

★

Only president whose son would
later become president

✪ PERSONAL ✪

Adams loved to take walks, go
fishing, and read. He was always
looking for new books to add
to his personal library.
Abigail Adams used to hang
laundry to dry in the East Room
of the White House.

★

I Told You We Should've Asked for Directions!

While going to Washington, D.C., to move into
the White House, John Adams and his family
got lost for several hours in the
woods north of the city.

★

Dot the i's and Cross the t's

After Thomas Jefferson finished
writing the Declaration of Independenc
John Adams had the task of revising it

THOMAS JEFFERSON

April 13, 1743 (Goochland [now Albemarle] County, Virginia) **Born**
July 4, 1826 (the same day John Adams died) **Died**
Democrat-Republican **Party**
Aaron Burr (1801-1805) and George Clinton (1805-1812) **Vice presidents**
6 feet 2 inches tall **Physical**
WIFE **Martha Skelton** DAUGHTERS **Martha ("Patsy") and Mary ("Polly")** **Family**

PRESIDENTIAL FIRSTS✪

First president to be inaugurated in Washington, D.C.

★
What Has Hundreds of Legs and Flies?

During the signing of the Declaration of Independence, which Jefferson wrote, the ceremony ended early because of all the flies that were bothering the members. Jefferson liked to say that it was under the "influence of flies" that the Declaration of Independence was voted upon.

✪ PERSONAL ✪

Jefferson was a well-educated man who spoke six languages. He was an architect, lawyer, musician, and inventor. He spent many long hours working to pass laws guaranteeing freedom of religion.

★
Nice Duds!

Thomas Jefferson liked to dress in his farmer clothes.

★
Friends 'Til the End

Thomas Jefferson and John Adams became very good friends after being president and wrote many letters to each other. They both died the same day, July 4, 1826, the 50th anniversary of the Declaration of Independence.

JAMES MADISON

Born March 16, 1751 (Port Conway, Virginia)
Died June 28, 1836
Party Democrat-Republican
Vice presidents George Clinton (1809-1812) and Elbridge Gerry (1813-1814)
Physical 5 feet 4 inches tall, 100 pounds
Family WIFE Dorothea ("Dolley") Payne Todd ("The Toast of Washington")

★ The Hostess with the Mostest

Dolley Madison was the official White House hostess for sixteen years for James Madison and Thomas Jefferson. She refused to leave the White House during the British invasion in 1812, insisting on staying until she knew her husband and many of the White House treasures were safe. In 1814, the Capitol and the "Executive Mansion" were burned by the British. The outside of the mansion was painted white, which is why it is known as the "White House."

✪ PERSONAL ✪

Madison played chess, rode horseback, and liked to read old Latin and Greek books.

★ Author, Author

James Madison is known as the "Father of the Constitution"—a name he hated. He was the main author of the Constitution and served as secretary of the conference that drafted it.

✪ PRESIDENTIAL FIRSTS ✪

First president to be younger than both his vice presidents and to have both vice presidents die while in office

First to lead troops and to face enemy fire while in office

First to wear long pants—the previous presidents wore knickers (very short pants)

JAMES MONROE

April 28, 1758 (Westmoreland County, Virginia) Born
July 4, 1831 Died
Democrat-Republican Party
Daniel Tompkins Vice president
A little over 6 feet tall Physical
WIFE Elizabeth Kortright DAUGHTERS Eliza and Maria Hester Family

PRESIDENT
5
1817-1825

✪ PRESIDENTIAL FIRSTS ✪

Only president to serve in two different cabinet posts
(secretary of state and secretary of war)

★

First president to tour the country

✪ PERSONAL ✪

Monroe was a friendly and
polite person. He loved to ride
horses and go hunting.

★

The Monroe Doctrine

President Monroe was worried
that foreign countries like
Spain and Russia would take
over areas that were important to the
United States. He warned other countries
against expansion in the Western half
of the world. This message came
to be called the Monroe Doctrine.

JOHN QUINCY ADAMS

PRESIDENT

6

1825-1829

Born July 11, 1767 (Braintree [now Quincy], Massachusetts)
Died February 23, 1848
Party Democrat-Republican
Vice president John C. Calhoun
Physical 5 feet 7 inches tall, 175 pounds
Family WIFE Louisa Catherine Johnson SONS George, John II, and Charles
FATHER John Adams (the second president)

✪ PERSONAL ✪

Adams woke up every morning at 5 a.m., built a †
read the Bible, and bathed in the Potomac Rive
He enjoyed reading, nature, horseback riding,
swimming, and going to the theater.

★
Skinny-Dipping

When John Quincy Adams was president he would take a morning walk down to the Potomac River and swim naked. One morning, a woman news reporter named Anne Royall sat on his clothes until he gave her an interview. He did the interview while standing chest deep in the Potomac.

✪ PRESIDENTIAL FIRSTS ✪

Only son of a president to become a president
★
First to have his photograph taken (1843)
★
Installed the first pool table in the White House

★
Man About the House

Adams is the only president to be elected to the House of Representatives after his term as president. (He served 17 years.)

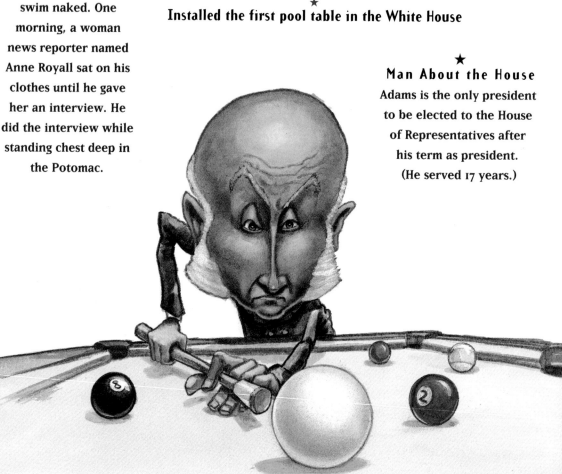

13

ANDREW JACKSON

h 15, 1767 (Waxhaw region between North and South Carolina) Born

June 8, 1845 Died

Democratic Party

John C. Calhoun (1829-1832), Martin Van Buren (1833-1837) Vice presidents

6 feet 1 inch tall, 145 pounds Physical

WIFE Rachel Donelson Robards SON Andrew Jr. [adopted nephew] Family

✪ PRESIDENTIAL FIRSTS ✪

First to survive an assassination attempt

★

Only president to help Congress pay off the national debt

★
Party Time

At Jackson's inaugural celebration, thousands of his supporters crashed e party at the White House. The farmers, woodsmen, and old soldiers tipped over tables, broke dishes, and climbed on furniture. To get rid of the crowd, waiters put giant tubs of punch on the White House lawn, luring people outside, and quickly locked the doors behind them.

★
Take That, You Brute!

On January 30, 1835, Richard Lawrence tried to assassinate Andrew Jackson. Both of Lawrence's guns misfired. Jackson chased after Lawrence, hitting him with his cane.

✪ PERSONAL ✪

Jackson was orphaned at 14 years of age. He was adopted by uneducated, hard-working parents. He was nicknamed "Old Hickory."

★
Mr. Veto

Jackson vetoed more bills than all the presidents before him combined.

MARTIN VAN BUREN

Born December 5, 1782 (Kinderhook, New York)

Died July 24, 1862

Party Democratic

Vice president Richard Mentor Johnson

Physical 5 feet 5 inches tall

Family WIFE Hannah Hoes SONS Abraham, John, Martin Jr., and Smith

PRESIDENT

8

1837-1841

★
Kissing Babies

Martin Van Buren was the country's first true politician president. He used speeches, rallies, sing-alongs, leaflets, and fund-raisers. He was known as the "Little Magician," because everything he touched turned into votes.

✪ PRESIDENTIAL FIRSTS ✪

First president born as a citizen of the United States: all the previous presidents were born before the Declaration of Independence, so they were born as British subjects.

★
I'm O.K., You're O.K.

Van Buren's nickname was Old Kinderhook. He approved things by signing "O.K." Many believe that is where the phrase "O.K." came from.

✪ PERSONAL ✪

Van Buren enjoyed attending the theater and the opera and going fishing.

WILLIAM HENRY HARRISON

February 9, 1773 (Charles City County, Virginia) Born
April 4, 1841 Died
Whig Party
John Tyler Vice president
5 feet 8 inches tall Physical
WIFE Anna Tuthill Symmes SONS John Cleves, William, John Scott, Benjamin, Family
and Carter DAUGHTERS Elizabeth, Lucy, Mary, and Anna

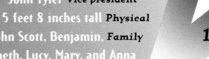

PRESIDENT

9

1841

✪ PERSONAL ✪

Harrison was 68 when he was inaugurated.
He enjoyed walking, horseback riding,
and reading the Bible.

★ Pets

"His Whiskers" was Harrison's goat.

★ Bundle Up

William Henry Harrison gave the longest **inaugural** speech in history, lasting over
one hour and 40 minutes. Harrison stood in a freezing cold March day without gloves,
hat, or coat. He caught a terrible cold, which turned to pneumonia and killed him on
April 4, 1841. He was president for only one month—the shortest term of any president.

✪ PRESIDENTIAL FIRSTS ✪

First president to die in office

JOHN TYLER

Born March 29, 1790 (Charles City County, Virginia)
Died January 18, 1862
Party Whig
Vice president None
Physical 6 feet tall.; very thin build
Family WIVES Letitia Christian [died 1842], Julia Gardiner ("The Rose of Long Island")
SONS Tazewell, John, Robert, David, John Alexander, Lachlan, Robert Fitzgerald,
and Lyon DAUGHTERS Alice, Letitia, Elizabeth, Mary, Anne, Julia, and Pearl

✪ PRESIDENTIAL FIRSTS ✪

First president to have no vice president
during an entire term

★ Pets

Tyler had a horse named
"General," a pet canary
named "Johnny Ty," and
an Italian greyhound
named "Le Beau."

★ Think of the Diapers

John Tyler had more children than any other
president—a grand total of 15.

✪ PERSONAL ✪

Tyler hunted fox and loved
wild animals. Tyler and his
wife, Julia, had some of the
greatest parties ever given
in the White House. Tyler
would play his violin
accompanied by Julia
on the guitar.

★ Too Many Vetoes?

In 1841, impeachment
proceedings were started
against Tyler for misusing
his veto power.

JAMES KNOX POLK

November 2, 1795 (Mecklenburg County, North Carolina) Born
June 15, 1849 Died
Democratic Party
George Mifflin Dallas Vice president
5 feet 8 inches tall Physical
WIFE Sarah Childress Family

PRESIDENT
11
1845-1849

★
I'll Buy Boardwalk

James Polk was known as the "real estate" president. During his term, the United States added 800,000 square miles of territory. He settled a boundary dispute with the British over the Oregon Territory. He also had the United States fight a war with Mexico to take the area in the Southwest that included New Mexico, Texas, and California.

✪ PRESIDENTIAL FIRSTS ✪
First president to voluntarily retire after one term

★
It's My Party...

James Polk wasn't a popular president. He and Mrs. Polk had some of the most boring parties ever to be thrown in the White House. Dancing and music were no-nos.

ZACHARY TAYLOR

Born November 24, 1784 (Orange County, Virginia)
Died July 9, 1850
Party Whig
Vice president Millard Fillmore
Physical 5 feet 8 inches tall, 170 pounds
Family WIFE Margaret ("Peggy") Mackall Smith SON Richard
DAUGHTERS Ann, Sarah, and Mary

✪ PRESIDENTIAL FIRSTS ✪

First president who never held a political office before the presidency

★

First to be elected from a state west of the Mississippi River (Louisiana)

★

Hey, Pal! Buy Yourself a Postcard

Taylor's faithful old war-horse, "Whitey," was allowed to graze on the White House front lawn. Some people say that tourists actually pulled hairs from Whitey's tail as souvenirs.

★

Old Rough and Ready

Before becoming president, Taylor was a general in the Army.

✪ PERSONAL ✪

Taylor was a very warm and personable man, although at times he was a little bit shy. He chewed tobacco and was famous for never missing a spittoon when he spat.

★

Seconds, Anyone?

Taylor spent an entire day at the Fourth of July ceremony laying the cornerstone of the Washington Monument. The day was scorching hot, and when the president got home, he ate giant helpings of cherries, iced milk, and pickled cucumbers, all while suffering from a case of typhus fever. He became quite ill and died five days later on July 9, 1850.

MILLARD FILLMORE

January 7, 1800 (Locke Township, Cayuga County, New York) Born
March 8, 1874 Died
Whig Party
None Vice president
6 feet tall Physical
WIFE Abigail Powers SON Millard DAUGHTER Mary Family

PRESIDENT
13
1850-1853

✪ PERSONAL ✪
Fillmore enjoyed collecting
books. He was nicknamed
"Last of the Whigs."

★
Book Him, Dano!
Millard Fillmore didn't go to school
when he was a child, so he didn't
know many words and could
barely read. He visited
a library in his town and
discovered a whole new world.
He enrolled at an academy in
New Hope, New York, where he
met and eventually married
teacher Abigail Powers. During
his presidency, Millard and
Abigail started the first permanent
library in the White House.
They had a personal library of
over 4,000 books.

✪ PRESIDENTIAL FIRSTS ✪
First president to have a stepmother
★
His wife, Abigail, had the first bathtub
with running water installed
in the White House.

FRANKLIN PIERCE

Born November 23, 1804 (Hillsborough, New Hampshire)
Died October 8, 1869
Party Democratic
Vice president William Rufus DeVane King
Physical 5 feet 10 inches tall
Family WIFE Jane Means Appleton SONS Franklin [died when three days old], Frank Rob‹
[died when four years old], and Benjamin [died in an accident two months
before the inauguration]

✪ PRESIDENTIAL FIRSTS ✪

First president whose vice president never served, because
he died before assuming any responsibilities

★

Only president to retain his original cabinet during his four years as president

★

First to put a Christmas tree in the White House

★

Kansas-Nebraska Act

The Kansas-Nebraska Act was strongly supported by Pierce. The Act let settlers in the Nebraska and Kansas territories decide for themselves whether to make slavery legal. People from the slave-state of Missouri illegally poured over the Kansas borders to vote in favor of slavery. The battles that took place because of the conflict generated the name "Bleeding Kansas." Opponents of the Act met in Wisconsin and started a new political force called the Republican Party.

✪ PERSONAL ✪

Pierce was an understanding person who made friends quite easily. He did, however, suffer from periods of depression and had a longtime battle with alcoholism. Pierce was an avid fisherman.

JAMES BUCHANAN

April 23, 1791 (Mercersburg, Pennsylvania) Born
June 1, 1868 Died
Democratic Party
John Cabell Breckinridge Vice-president
6 feet tall Physical
Buchanan was never married. Harriet Lane, his niece, served as hostess. Family

PRESIDENT

15

1857-1861

✪ PERSONAL ✪
Buchanan enjoyed reading, playing cards, and entertaining his friends. When he talked to people he tipped his head to the left and closed one eye because one of his eyes was farsighted while the other was nearsighted. To make the matter worse, his left eye sat a bit higher in the socket.

✪ PRESIDENTIAL FIRSTS ✪
First president to send a transatlantic telegram: on August 16, 1858, he exchanged greetings with Queen Victoria of Great Britain.

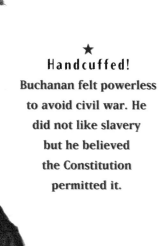

★ Good Riddance
Buchanan sent a note to newly elected President Abraham Lincoln stating, "My dear sir, If you are as happy on entering the White House as I on leaving, you are a happy man indeed."

★ Handcuffed!
Buchanan felt powerless to avoid civil war. He did not like slavery but he believed the Constitution permitted it.

22

★
Spy vs. Spy
Lincoln's wife, Mary, had
four brothers and four
brothers-in-law who
fought for the South
during the Civil War.
There were many rumors
throughout Washington,
D.C., that Mary Lincoln
was a Confederate spy.
Abe was so distressed by
these rumors that he
appeared personally at a
Senate hearing to denounce
the rumors.

★
Nickname
Honest Abe

★
Favorite Food
Fricasseed chicken

LINCOLN

February 12, 1809 (Hodgenville, Hardin [now Larue] County, Kentucky) *Born*

April 15, 1865 *Died*

Republican *Party*

Hannibal Hamlin (1861-1865) and Andrew Johnson (1865) *Vice presidents*

6 feet 4 inches tall (he was the tallest president), 180 pounds *Physical*

WIFE **Mary Todd** SONS **Robert, William ("Willie"), and Thomas ("Tad")** *Family*

✪ PRESIDENTIAL FIRSTS ✪

First president to be photographed at his inauguration (his second, in 1865).
In the photo, John Wilkes Booth can be seen standing close to Lincoln.
(John Wilkes Booth assassinated Lincoln in 1865.)

✪ PERSONAL ✪

Lincoln liked to read, go to the theater, play chess,
and share stories and jokes with his friends.
He also spent a good many hours splitting wood.
He was a man of great character and suffered a great
deal personally to keep the United States united.

★ Did'ya Hear the One About the...

Abraham Lincoln loved to tell jokes,
poems, and stories. He was quite famous
during his time for replying to questions
with "That reminds me of a story." Lincoln
laughed and joked about politics, the Civil
War, and even himself. Lincoln was not
considered very good-looking. When
Senator Stephen Douglas called him a
"two-faced man," Lincoln replied: "I
leave it to my audience. If I had another
face, do you think I would wear this one?"

★ What Happened?

1861—1865 - Civil War
1861 - Virginia, Arkansas,
Alabama, Florida, Georgia,
Louisiana, Mississippi, South
Carolina, Texas, Tennessee,
and North Carolina secede
from the U.S. to form the
Confederate States of America.
1863 - Emancipation
Proclamation - Lincoln
frees the slaves
1863 - Gettysburg Address
1865 - Confederate General
Robert E. Lee surrenders at
Appomattox Courthouse.
1865 - Lincoln assassinated by
John Wilkes Booth.

★ Pets

"Bob," a gray and white Maltese cat; "Jack," the Lincoln family's pet turkey,
who was saved by the Lincoln boys from Thanksgiving dinner;
and "Jib," a mongrel dog who would often sit on Abe's lap and eat table scraps.

ANDREW JOHNSON

Born December 29, 1808 (Raleigh, North Carolina)
Died July 31, 1875
Party Democratic
Vice president None
Physical 5 feet 10 inches tall
Family WIFE Eliza McCardle SONS Charles, Robert, and Andrew DAUGHTERS Martha and M

★
Have I Got a Deal for You!

In 1867, the United States bought the Alaska Territory from Russia for $7.2 million. The people living in Alaska were given three years to decide whether they wanted to stay in Alaska or move back to Russia.

✪ PRESIDENTIAL FIRSTS ✪

Only president to be impeached

★

First visit by a queen – Queen Emma, of the Sandwi Islands (Hawaii) – to an American president, on August 14, 1866

✪ PERSONAL ✪

Johnson was a great speaker. He liked the circus and minstrel shows, vegetable gardening, and playing checkers.

★
A Stitch in Time

When Andrew Johnson was 14, he and his brother were sold as servants to a tailor. The boys had to work for the tailor, who in turn gave them food, clothing, and shelter, and taught them how to be tailors. After two years the boys ran away. The tailor ran an ad offering a $10 reward for their return, but the boys were never caught.

ULYSSES SIMPSON GRANT

April 27, 1822 (Point Pleasant, Ohio) **Born**
July 23, 1885 **Died**
Republican **Party**
Schuyler Colfax (1869-1873) and Henry Wilson (1873-1875) **Vice presidents**
5 feet 7 inches tall **Physical**
WIFE **Julia Boggs Dent** SONS **Frederick, Ulysses ("Buck"), and Jesse** Family
DAUGHTER **Ellen ("Nellie")**

PRESIDENT
18
1869-1877

★
License and Registration, Please

Grant was riding his racing horse one day in downtown Washington, D.C., when a police officer gave him a ticket for speeding. The officer didn't recognize the president and fined him $20. The president paid his $20 fine and sent a commendation to the officer.

✪ PRESIDENTIAL FIRSTS ✪

First president to have both parents alive when taking office

★
**First presidential candidate to have a female opponent
(Victoria Claflin Woodhull)**

✪ PERSONAL ✪

Grant was a West Point graduate and the commanding general of the Union Army the end of the Civil War. He liked to smoke cigars, race horses, draw, and paint.

★
The Name Game

Grant's original name was Hiram Ulysses Grant. When he was accepted to West Point, he didn't want the initials H.U.G. labeled on his possessions, so he switched his name to Ulysses Hiram Grant. When he got to school, he found he was registered by the name Ulysses Simpson Grant. He liked the name and kept it.

★
Favorite Breakfast
Cucumbers soaked in vinegar

RUTHERFORD BIRCHARD HAYES

Born October 4, 1822 (Delaware, Ohio)
Died January 17, 1893
Party Republican
Vice president William Almon Wheeler
Physical 5 feet 7 inches tall, 175 pounds
Family WIFE Lucy Ware Webb SONS Sardis, James, Rutherford Platt, and Scott
DAUGHTER Frances ("Fanny")

✪ PERSONAL ✪

Hayes was serious, honest, and hardworking.
He enjoyed the outdoors, reading, playing chess, and landscaping his home grounds.

✪ PRESIDENTIAL FIRSTS ✪

First president to use the telephone

★

First to visit the West Coast while in office

★

Only president elected after losing the popular vote
(see how a president is elected on page 54)

★
Hey, Kid! Get Off My Lawn

First Lady Lucy Hayes started the traditional annual Easter Egg Roll at the White House. The event had been held on the Capitol lawn, but Congress complained that the event ruined the grass.

★
Thirsty?

"Lemonade Lucy" was the nickname given to Lucy Hayes because she wouldn't allow any alcohol to be served in the White House. She also didn't allow any smoking, dancing, or card playing.

(see how a president is elected on page 54)

JAMES ABRAM GARFIELD

November 19, 1831 (Orange, Cuyahoga County, Ohio) Born
September 19, 1881 Died
Republican Party
Chester Alan Arthur Vice president
6 feet tall, 185 pounds Physical
WIFE Lucretia ("Crete") Rudolph SONS Harry, James, Irvin, and Abram Family
DAUGHTER Mary

PRESIDENT
20
1881

★
Quit Horsing Around

When he was a boy, James Garfield worked on
the Erie Canal. He led the horses that pulled the
floatboat *Evening Star* on the bank of the river. He was dunked quite
a few times before he finally got the horses to cooperate.

✪ PRESIDENTIAL FIRSTS ✪

First left-handed president

★

**First to campaign in more than one language
(English and Spanish)**

✪ PERSONAL ✪

Garfield was a friendly
person who liked
to hug people or put
his arm around
whomever he
was talking to.
He enjoyed playing
chess and billiards
and could write
with either hand.

★
Assassination

James Garfield was shot on July 2,
1881, in a Baltimore railroad
station. Charles J. Guiteau had
been stalking the president for
weeks but had never had the
nerve to shoot him until July 2.
Guiteau used a .44 British Bulldog
pistol because he thought "it
would look nice in a museum
someday." Garfield lived for 80
days after he was shot.

CHESTER ALAN ARTHUR

Born October 5, 1830 (North Fairfield, Vermont)
Died November 18, 1886
Party Republican
Vice president None
Physical 6 feet 2 inches tall, 220 pounds
Family WIFE Ellen ("Nell") Lewis Herndon SON Chester Jr. DAUGHTER Ellen ("Nell")

✪ PRESIDENTIAL FIRSTS ✪

First president to have his citizenship questioned
(many people believed he was born in Canada)

★

First to take the oath of office in his own home

Favorite Food
Mutton chops

This Is a Test–This Is Only a Test

During Chester Arthur's time as president, a change in the civil service (government jobs) took place. A test was now to be given to those people wanting government jobs. This would make sure that the jobs were given to the people most qualified instead of the people doing favors for the politicians in charge of giving the jobs.

✪ PERSONAL ✪

To lighten the mood of the country after the serious personality of President Hayes and the sadness over President Garfield's assassination, Arthur redecorated the White House and entertained the people of Washington, D.C. He was a romantic gentleman who liked to fish and hunt.

STEPHEN GROVER CLEVELAND

March 18, 1837 (Caldwell, New Jersey) Born
June 24, 1908 Died
Democratic Party
Thomas Andrews Hendricks Vice president
5 feet 11 inches tall, 250 pounds Physical
WIFE Frances Folsom SONS Richard and Francis Family
DAUGHTERS Ruth, Esther, and Marion

★

But How Many Home Runs Did She Hit?

Some people think that the Baby Ruth candy bar was named after Cleveland's
first daughter, Ruth. During Cleveland's first term, Ruth would play on the
White House front lawn. She had to stop playing out front because
too many tourists would pick her up and pass her around.

✪ PERSONAL ✪

Cleveland was known as an honest and good man. He
was also quick-tempered and blunt. His favorite
sport was fishing. He also liked to play
cards and eat German food.

★

Honesty Is the Best Policy

Cleveland was known for his honesty.
When he came to Washington, D.C., he
began cleaning up the corruption that had
occurred before he was president. He
reviewed the records of many government
employees and fired them if there was
evidence of wrongdoing.

✪ PRESIDENTIAL FIRSTS ✪

Only president elected to two nonconsecutive terms (1885-1889 and 1893-1897)

★

Only president to be married in the White House and first to have a child born there

BENJAMIN HARRISON

Born August 20, 1833 (North Bend, Ohio)
Died March 13, 1901
Party Republican
Vice president Levi Parsons Morton
Physical 5 feet 6 inches tall
Family WIVES Caroline Lavinia Scott [died 1892], Mary Lord Dimmick SON Russell Benjamin DAUGHTERS Mary Scott ("Mamie") and Elizabeth

✪ PRESIDENTIAL FIRSTS ✪
Only grandson of a president to be elected to the presidency

★ You Light Up My Life
In 1891, the Edison Electric company installed the first electricity in the White House. After Benjamin Harrison got an electrical shock, the family often refused to touch the light switches. Sometimes the Harrison family went to bed leaving on all the lights in the White House.

★ Sooner or Later
When the Oklahoma Territory was opened up for expansion, settlers would race from designated areas at set times to claim plots of free land for their families. Some people cheated and left before they were supposed to. The cheating settlers became known as "Sooners."

✪ PERSONAL ✪
Harrison was known as the "Human Iceberg" because he was stiff and formal when dealing with people. He was very smart and paid attention to details.

★ Following in Grandpa's Footsteps
Benjamin Harrison's grandfather was William Henry Harrison, the ninth president.

STEPHEN GROVER CLEVELAND

March 18, 1837 (Caldwell, New Jersey) Born
June 24, 1908 Died
Democratic Party
Adlai E. Stevenson Vice president
5 feet 11 inches tall, 250 pounds Physical
WIFE Frances Folsom SONS Richard and Francis Family
DAUGHTERS Ruth, Esther, and Marion

PRESIDENT
24
1893-1897

★
A Three-Hour Cruise, a Three-Hour Cruise

Grover Cleveland went sailing in July 1893 for what many people thought was a fishing trip on the private yacht *Oneida*. But the trip was not for fishing. Cleveland secretly had surgery for a cancerous growth in his mouth. The operation was so secret that nobody found out about it until 1917 when one of the doctors let the secret slip out.

✪ PRESIDENTIAL FIRSTS ✪

**Only president elected to two nonconsecutive terms
(1885-1889 and 1893-1897)**

★
Veto, Veto

During his two terms, Grover Cleveland used his veto power 584 times. This is the highest total of any president except Franklin Roosevelt.

★
Burning the Midnight Oil

Grover Cleveland was known for working extremely hard. Many times he could be found working well into the early morning hours.

WILLIAM MCKINLEY

Born January 29, 1843 (Niles, Ohio)
Died September 14, 1901
Party Republican
Vice presidents Garret Augustus Hobart (1897-1899) and Theodore Roosevelt (190
Physical 5 feet 7 inches tall, 190 to 200 pounds
Family WIFE Ida Saxton DAUGHTERS Katherine ("Katie") and Ida [both died as babies]

✪ PRESIDENTIAL FIRSTS ✪
First president to campaign by telephone

★ Aloha!
In 1898, William McKinley signed a joint congressional resolution annexing (annexing means to add or to join to something bigger) the Hawaiian Islands.

✪ PERSONAL ✪
McKinley was a cheerful and friendly man loved by almost everyone. He enjoyed the opera, the theater, and cribbage.

Greetings From **HAWAII**

★ Assassination
In 1901, William McKinley was shot by Leon Czolgosz after giving a speech in Buffalo, New York. He lived for eight days after being shot.

★ Tie a Purple Ribbon 'Round the Ol' Oak Tree
William McKinley's wife, Ida, couldn't stand the color yellow. She banned anything yellow from being in the White House. She even ordered the gardeners to pull up all the yellow flowers.

THEODORE ROOSEVELT

October 27, 1858 (New York, New York) Born
January 6, 1919 Died
Republican Party
Charles Warren Fairbanks (1905-1909) Vice president
5 feet 8 inches tall, 200 pounds Physical
WIVES Alice Hathaway Lee [died 1884], Edith Kermit Carow Family
SONS Theodore Jr., Kermit, Archibald Bulloch, and Quentin
DAUGHTERS Alice and Ethel Carow

PRESIDENT
26
1901-1909

✪ PERSONAL ✪

Roosevelt was one of the most colorful presidents in U.S. history. He rode horseback, hunted, and boxed (even as president!). He wrote books about politics, America, outdoor pastimes, wilderness, and great adventures. The "teddy bear" was named after him in 1903, and his favorite word was "Bully!"– which meant *great*.

★
Dig, Dig, Dig

Roosevelt began the construction of the Panama Canal, which cost $400 million and took 43,000 workers to complete. It was finished in 1914. It is the easiest and shortest route for ships to travel between the Atlantic and Pacific oceans.

✪ PRESIDENTIAL FIRSTS ✪

First president to win a
Nobel Peace Prize (in 1906)
★
First to visit a foreign
country while in office
★
First to ride in a car, to ride
in a submarine, and to fly
in a plane (on October 11,
1910, he flew for four
minutes in a plane built
by the Wright brothers).

WILLIAM HOWARD TAFT

PRESIDENT

27

1909-1913

Born **September 15, 1857 (Cincinnati, Ohio)**
Died **March 8, 1930**
Party **Republican**
Vice president **James Schoolcraft Sherman**
Physical **6 feet 2 inches tall, 300-350 pounds**
Family WIFE **Helen ("Nellie") Herron** SONS **Robert Alphonso and Charles Phelps**
DAUGHTER **Helen Herron**

✪ PRESIDENTIAL FIRSTS ✪

First president of all 48 connecting states

★

First to serve on the U.S. Supreme Court

★

First to throw a ceremonial first pitch at a baseball game

★ But Honey, I Wanna Be a Judge

William Taft never really wanted to be president. He wanted to be Chief Justice of the U.S. Supreme Court. His wife, however, wanted to be first lady, and talked him into running for president. In 1921, Taft got his wish and became the Chief Justice.

★ Pets

The Tafts kept their Holstein cow, "Pauline Wayne," on the White House front lawn.

★ Big Bill

William Taft was the largest man ever to be president. Once he actually got stuck in a White House bathtub. After he was helped free, he ordered the installation of a special oversized bathtub, which could hold four normal-sized men.

✪ PERSONAL ✪

Taft was a very popular man with a cheerful personality and a wonderful sense of humor. He enjoyed playing golf and watching baseball. He was also a good dancer and tennis player.

THOMAS WOODROW WILSON

December 28, 1856 (Staunton, Virginia) Born
February 3, 1924 Died
Democratic Party
Thomas Riley Marshall Vice president
5 feet 11 inches tall Physical
WIVES Ellen Louise Axson [died 1914], Edith Bolling Galt Family
DAUGHTERS Margaret Woodrow, Jessie Woodrow, and Eleanor Randolph

PRESIDENT
28
1913–1921

✪ PERSONAL ✪

Wilson loved to attend the theater, especially vaudeville.

★ Not in Their League

One of Wilson's most important projects was the founding of the League of Nations. It was to be a large group of countries that would help settle arguments between countries to avoid wars. The U.S. Congress voted to not join the League of Nations. Without the United States, the League of Nations was never as powerful as planned.

★ Madame President

Toward the end of his presidency, Wilson suffered a stroke which paralyzed his left side. During his recovery, his wife, Edith, was his connection to the outside world. There probably hasn't been a more powerful first lady than Edith Wilson was during this time.

✪ PRESIDENTIAL FIRSTS ✪

First president to have earned a Ph.D.

★ First to cross the Atlantic while in office

★ Pets

Wilson had a sheep named "Old Ike" that chewed tobacco and grazed on the White House front lawn.

★ The War to End All Wars

World War I was fought from 1914 to 1918. The U.S. reluctantly joined the war against Germany in 1917 because German submarines would not stop sinking U.S. ships.

WARREN GAMALIEL HARDING

Born November 2, 1865 (Corsica, Ohio)
Died August 2, 1923
Party Republican
Vice president John Calvin Coolidge
Physical 6 feet tall
Family WIFE Florence Kling De Wolfe   DAUGHTER Elizabeth Ann Christian

✪ PRESIDENTIAL FIRSTS ✪

First president to visit Alaska

★

First to ride to his inauguration in a car

★

First to give a national speech over the radio

★ Hit Me!

Warren Harding would play poker at least twice a week. Once he gambled away an entire set of White House china dishes dating back to Benjamin Harrison. President Harding's political advisors were even given the nickname of the "Poker Cabinet."

★ We Can't All Be Perfect

During Harding's presidency, numerous scandals took place involving members of his staff. Secretary of the Interior Albert Fall, for example, sold for his own profit the country's oil reserves at Wyoming's Teapot Dome.

★ Pets

The Hardings had a canary named "Bob" and a dog named "Laddie Boy," which once had a birthday party in the White House.

★ Died in Office

Harding died of a heart attack while president.

✪ PERSONAL ✪

Harding tried to please other people and avoid confrontation. He enjoyed playing golf and poker.

JOHN CALVIN COOLIDGE

July 4, 1872 (Plymouth, Vermont) Born
January 5, 1933 Died
Republican Party
Charles Gates Dawes (1925-1929) Vice president
5 feet 9 inches tall Physical
WIFE Grace Anna Goodhue SONS John and Calvin Family

PRESIDENT
30
1923-1929

★ Hey, Dad! Wake Up!

Vice president Coolidge was on vacation at his father's house when he learned that President Harding had died. At 2:47 a.m. on August 3, 1923, Coolidge was sworn into office by his father, John Coolidge, who was a justice of the peace. President Coolidge then went back to sleep.

★ Hi Ho, Nuts and Bolts! Away!

Coolidge had an electronic horse installed in the White House, and he would ride it almost every day.

✪ PERSONAL ✪

Calvin Coolidge enjoyed being photographed while wearing Indian headdresses and Boy Scout uniforms.

✪ PRESIDENTIAL FIRSTS ✪

First president to be sworn in by his father

★

First to have been born on the Fourth of July

★ Pets

The Coolidge family had dogs and cats, as well as a donkey named "Ebeneezer," a goose that had starred in a Broadway play, and a raccoon named "Rebecca." Occasionally, Coolidge was found walking around the White House with Rebecca on his shoulders.

Born **August 10, 1874 (West Branch, Iowa)**
Died **October 20, 1964**
Party **Republican**
Vice president **John Charles Curtis**
Physical **5 feet 11 inches tall**
Family WIFE **Lou Henry** SONS **Herbert Jr. and Allan**

✪ PERSONAL ✪

Hoover was a hardworking man who was a bit shy and uncomfortable in crowds. He would exercise every morning by throwing a medicine ball around for 30 minutes.

✪ PRESIDENTIAL FIRSTS ✪

First president born west of the Mississippi River

★

Approved "The Star-Spangled Banner" as the national anthem

★

Hey, Buddy, Can You Spare a Dime?

Herbert Hoover was president when the Great Depression took place. Hundreds of thousands of people lost their jobs and struggled to feed their families. Hoover was sad to see people cold and hungry, but he felt the government should not interfere with business. Even though it really wasn't his fault, Hoover was blamed for the Great Depression. Slums were called "Hoovervilles" and newspapers worn for warmth were called "Hoover blankets."

FRANKLIN DELANO ROOSEVELT

January 30, 1882 (Hyde Park, New York) Born
April 12, 1945 Died
Democratic Party
John Nance Garner (1933-41), Henry Agard Wallace (1941-45), Vice presidents
Harry S. Truman (1945)
6 feet 1 inch tall, 180 pounds Physical
WIFE Eleanor ("The First Lady of the World") Roosevelt (his fifth cousin) Family
SONS James, Elliott, Franklin Delano Jr., and John DAUGHTER Anna Eleanor

PRESIDENT
★32★
1933-1945

✪ PERSONAL ✪

Roosevelt contracted polio and became paralyzed
in 1921. He swam to get his strength back.
He wasn't sensitive about his disability,
and often joked about it to make other
people more comfortable.

★ A Day That Will Live in Infamy

On December 7, 1941, the Japanese bombed Pearl Harbor
in Hawaii, killing 2,300 Americans and wounding 1,200
more. The next day, Roosevelt asked Congress for a
declaration of war. With American support, the Allies
(Great Britain, Canada, Russia, and France) were able
to defeat the Axis powers (Germany, Japan, and Italy)
in 1945 to end World War II.

★ All in the Family

Franklin's fifth
cousin was Theodore
Roosevelt, the
twenty-sixth president.

✪ PRESIDENTIAL FIRSTS ✪

First president whose mother was
eligible to vote for him

★

First to be elected to more than two terms
(he was elected four terms)

★

First to appear on television

★ It's a Dog Eat Dog Presidency

Roosevelt had a dog named "Fala" that was with
him all the time. Reporters called Fala, "Fala
the informer" because wherever the dog was,
Roosevelt was not far behind. Roosevelt also
had a German shepherd named "Major" that
was famous for biting several politicians.

HARRY S. TRUMAN

PRESIDENT 33

1945-1953

Born May 8, 1884 (Lamar, Missouri)
Died December 26, 1972
Party Democratic
Vice president Alben William Barkley (1949-1953)
Physical 5 feet 10 inches tall, 185 pounds
Family WIFE Elizabeth ("Bess") Virginia Wallace DAUGHTER Margaret

✪ PRESIDENTIAL FIRSTS ✪
First president to give a speech on TV

★
OOPS!

On election day, 1948, the *Chicago Tribune* made a big mistake when it reported that Republican Thomas Dewey, not Truman, was the winner of the presidential election.

★
All Aboard!

During the 1948 presidential campaign, Harry Truman took a 30,000-mile whistle-stop tour of the United States. At each stop, many people would come to listen to Truman's speech. Many supporters would yell, "Give 'em hell, Harry!" The tour may have been the event that turned voters to Truman's favor.

★
The Buck Stops Here!

In his first six months as president, Truman brought an end to World War II, which included dropping two atomic bombs on Japan. He also prevented the expansion of communism and helped start the United Nations.

✪ PERSONAL ✪
Truman loved to play cards, horseshoes, and the piano.

DWIGHT DAVID EISENHOWER

October 14, 1890 (Denison, Texas) **Born**
March 28, 1969 **Died**
Republican Party
Richard M. Nixon **Vice president**
5 feet 10 inches tall, 178 pounds **Physical**
WIFE Mamie Geneva Doud **SON** John Sheldon **Family**

P R E S I D E N T
34
1953-1961

✪ PERSONAL ✪

Eisenhower was superstitious. He carried three coins in his pocket for good luck: a silver dollar, a five-guinea gold piece, and a French franc. He was a wonderful chef, who specialized in barbecued steaks. His nickname was "Ike."

★ Supreme Commander

In World War II, General Eisenhower was in charge of all the troops fighting in Europe for America and its allies.

★ Favorite Dessert

Prune whip

★ Bombs Away!

During Eisenhower's presidency, the United States started to build up gigantic numbers of nuclear missiles in the hopes that the Soviet Union would think twice before using its nuclear weapons against us.

✪ PRESIDENTIAL FIRSTS ✪

First president of all 50 states

★

First to appear on color television

★ Green With Envy

Eisenhower's favorite game was golf. He liked it so much that the United States Golf Association built a putting green near the White House so he could practice any time he wanted.

JOHN FITZGERALD KENNEDY

Born May 29, 1917 (Brookline, Massachusetts)
Died November 22, 1963
Party Democratic
Vice president Lyndon B. Johnson
Physical 6 feet tall, 170 pounds
Family WIFE Jacqueline Lee Bouvier SONS John Jr. and Patrick [died as a baby]
DAUGHTER Caroline

✪ PERSONAL ✪

President Kennedy thought his best quality was his curiosity and his worst was his irritability.
His charm, grace, and wit made him popular. He is remembered for the quotation,
"Ask not what your country can do for you, ask what you can do for your country."

★
One of These Days... Pow! Right to the Moon!

President Kennedy set a goal for the United States of putting a man on the moon
by the end of the decade. During Kennedy's term, the National Aeronautics and
Space Administration (NASA) started testing the effects of weightlessness in space
and of re-entry on human pilots. Astronauts Neil Armstrong and Buzz Aldrin
walked on the moon on July 20, 1969.

✪ PRESIDENTIAL FIRSTS ✪

**First to have won a Pulitzer Prize
(for the book *Profiles in Courage*)**

★
Assassination

John Kennedy was shot
by Lee Harvey Oswald on
November 22, 1963.

LYNDON BAINES JOHNSON

August 27, 1908 (Stonewall, Texas) Born
January 22, 1973 Died
Democratic Party
Hubert Horatio Humphrey (1965-1969) Vice president
6 feet 3 inches tall, 210 pounds Physical
WIFE Claudia Alta ("Lady Bird") Taylor   DAUGHTERS Lynda Bird and Family
Luci Baines (All of the Johnsons had the initials "LBJ.")

PRESIDENT
36
1963-1969

✪ PRESIDENTIAL FIRSTS ✪

rst president to have the oath of office administered by a woman

★

First to take the oath of office in an airplane

✪ PERSONAL ✪

Johnson was very competitive.
One of his favorite activities was
to take visitors on 90-mile-per-hour
rides around his Texas ranch in
his Lincoln Continental.

★ The Great Society

Johnson wanted to be
emembered for turning America
into the "Great Society"—a
place without ignorance,
poverty, and racial injustice.
Unfortunately, Johnson is
most remembered for the
Vietnam War, which was so
negative that he didn't run
for re-election.

★ Pets

"Him" and "Her" were the Johnsons' pet beagles.
Him's paw prints are imprinted in cement in the
walkway leading to the White House press room.
FBI director J. Edgar Hoover gave Johnson
a beagle named "Edgar."

★ Favorite Foods

Canned green peas and tapioca

RICHARD MILHOUS NIXON

Born January 9, 1913 (Yorba Linda, California)
Died April 22, 1994
Party Republican
Vice presidents Spiro T. Agnew (1969-1973) and Gerald R. Ford (1973-1974)
Physical 5 feet 11 inches tall, 175 pounds
Family WIFE Thelma Catherine Patricia ("Pat") Ryan DAUGHTERS Patricia ("Tricia") and Julie

★ Watergate

Some of the people that Nixon hired to help him as president were found guilty of wrongdoings that came to be known as the "Watergate scandals." These wrongdo included planting of listening devices in the Democratic office at the Watergate bui In 1974, impeachment proceedings began against President Nixon for covering u the Watergate scandals. When Nixon realized that he faced almost certain impeachment, he decided to resign.

★ Ping-Pong Diplomacy

In 1972, Richard Nixon took "A Journey for Peace." He traveled to China to meet with Chairman Mao Tse-Tung in hopes of broadening scientific, cultural, and trade contacts.

✪ PRESIDENTIAL FIRSTS ✪
First president to visit China while in offic

✪ PERSONAL ✪
Nixon suffered from motion sickness and hay fever.

GERALD RUDOLPH FORD

July 14, 1913 (Omaha, Nebraska) Born
Republican Party
Nelson A. Rockefeller Vice president
6 feet tall, 195 pounds Physical
WIFE Elizabeth Anne ("Betty") Bloomer Warren SONS Michael Gerald, Family
John ("Jack"), and Steven Meigs DAUGHTER Susan Elizabeth

PRESIDENT
38
1974-1977

✪ PRESIDENTIAL FIRSTS ✪

First to be appointed as vice president under the 25th Amendment
to the Constitution, when Spiro T. Agnew resigned in 1973

★

Only president to serve without being chosen in a national election

★
Helpful Hand

n an effort to bring an end
to a period of conflict
in America, Ford pardoned
ormer President Nixon for
Watergate and offered
clemency to draft dodgers
and deserters from the
Vietnam War.

★
Good Sport

Gerald Ford was on the University of Michigan
football team from 1931 to 1934. In 1935, he played
in a college all-star game against the Chicago
Bears. He was offered tryouts by both the Green
Bay Packers and the Detroit Lions. While he was
in office, Ford continued to participate in
athletics, and enjoyed swimming, lifting weights,
skiing, and playing golf. In 1977, he had a
hole-in-one at the Memphis Classic.

✪ PERSONAL ✪

Ford is considered to be the most
athletic president to occupy the
White House. He is a right-handed
sportsman, yet he writes and
eats with his left hand.

JAMES EARL CARTER

Born October 1, 1924 (Plains, Georgia)
Party Democratic
Vice president Walter Mondale
Physical 5 feet 9 inches tall, 155 pounds
Family WIFE Eleanor Rosalynn Smith SONS John, James, and Jeffrey DAUGHTER Amy

★ **Favorite Foods**
Mixed nuts
and peaches

✪ **PERSONAL** ✪
Carter studied nuclear physics at the Naval Academy.
He liked to wear denim "peanut clothes" and often wore
his "lucky" red tie.

★ **A Little Light Reading**
Jimmy Carter is a speed-reader. He has been
recorded reading 2,000 words a minute. It
was common for him to read two or three
books a week while he was president.

✪ **PRESIDENTIAL FIRSTS** ✪
First president to graduate from Annapolis
(the U.S. Naval Academy)

★ **Creamy or Chunky**
In 1953, Jimmy Carter returned from the Navy to Plains, Georgia, to take over the peanut farm
left by his late father. He improved production and expanded the scale of the farm so that it
became a thriving business. By 1979, he had become a millionaire in the peanut industry.

RONALD WILSON REAGAN

February 6, 1911 (Tampico, Illinois) Born
Republican Party
George Bush Vice president
6 feet 1 inch tall, 185 pounds Physical
WIVES Jane Wyman [divorced 1948], Nancy Davis Family
SONS Michael and Ronald Jr. DAUGHTERS Maureen and Patti

PRESIDENT

40

1981-1989

✪ PRESIDENTIAL FIRSTS ✪

Only president to have been divorced

★

First to be wounded by and to survive an assassination attempt

★

Only president to be inaugurated after his 70th birthday

★

Favorite Foods

Lasagna, macaroni and
cheese, and jelly beans
(his favorite jelly bean
flavor is coconut)

★

Lights, Camera, Action

Reagan was a successful actor before he entered politics. He
acted in such television shows and movies as *Knute Rockne, All
American; Death Valley Days; Bedtime for Bonzo;* and a 1958
production called *A Turkey for President.*

✪ PERSONAL ✪

Reagan is known as the "Great Communicator"
because he used television so well to
present his policies and programs.
He enjoys working on his ranch
in California clearing brush, building
fences, and chopping wood.

GEORGE HERBERT WALKER BUSH

Born June 12, 1924 (Milton, Massachusetts)
Party Republican
Vice president James Danforth Quayle
Physical 6 feet 2 inches tall, 195 pounds
Family WIFE Barbara Pierce SONS George, John ("Jeb"), Neil, and Marvin
DAUGHTERS Dorothy ("Doro") and Robin [died of leukemia at age four]

★ Desert Storm

On August 2, 1990, Iraq invaded the country of Kuwait. Bush ordered operation Desert Shield—a series of diplomatic action and embargoes. Desert Shield failed to work, so operation Desert Storm was started on January 17, 1991. Desert Storm involved massive bombing and ground attacks. American troops liberated Kuwait City, the capital of Kuwait. The war lasted until President Bush called for a cease-fire on February 27, 1991.

★ Tumbling Down

The Berlin Wall, a symbol of the Cold War erected in 1961, was taken down on Novemeber 9, 1989.

★ Eat Your Vegetables, George

Broccoli farmers were upset when George Bush said that he did not like broccoli. The farmers sent truckloads of broccoli to the White House. Barbara Bush graciously accepted the broccoli, but President Bush said, "I am President of the United States and I don't have to eat it."

✪ PERSONAL ✪

Bush is a quiet, gentle man who would much rather talk than fight. He played first base for the Yale baseball team.

WILLIAM JEFFERSON CLINTON

August 19, 1946 (Hope, Arkansas) **Born**
Democratic Party
Albert Gore Vice president
6 feet 1 inch tall, 200 pounds Physical
WIFE **Hillary Rodham** DAUGHTER **Chelsea** Family

PRESIDENT
42
1993-present

✪ PRESIDENTIAL FIRSTS ✪

First president to have been a Rhodes scholar

✪ PERSONAL ✪

Clinton is the first "baby boomer" president. During his campaign he got a reputation for enjoying fast food and r being an avid jogger. In 1963, when Bill Clinton was 16 years old, he was a member of the Arkansas group to the Boy's Nation program. The highlight was a meeting at the White House with then- President John Kennedy.

★
Pet
"Socks" the cat

★
Favorite Ice Cream
Mango

★
Great Sax
Bill Clinton plays both the tenor and the soprano saxophone. During his campaign, he made many appearances playing the saxophone, entertaining voters all across America.

★
Favorite Sandwich
Peanut butter and banana

Washington

J. Adams

Jefferson

Madison

Monroe

J. Q. Adams

Jackson

Van Buren

W. Harrison

Tyler

Polk

Taylor

Fillmore

Pierce

Buchanan

Lincoln

A. Johnson

Grant

Hayes

Garfield

Arthur

Cleveland

B. Harrison

McKinley

T. Roosevelt

Taft

Wilson

Harding

Coolidge

Hoover

F. Roosevelt

Truman

Eisenhower

Kennedy

L. Johnson

Nixon

Ford

Carter

Reagan

Bush

Clinton

WHAT DOES A PRESIDENT DO?

The president acts both as a political leader and as a symbol of our nation. He or she is the "chief executive" in charge of enforcing the laws of the country and running the executive branch of the government. He or she is commander in chief of the military. The president works with the Senate and the House of Representatives. He or she negotiates treaties with other countries and appoints judges, ambassadors, and other high government officials. The president can veto legislation proposed by Congress, while it takes the approval of the president and the entire Congress to pass legislation. (A veto may be overridden if the Senate and the House of Representatives both vote with a two-thirds majority.)

The Constitution outlines five areas that make up the president's job description:

1. Commander In Chief

The president is in charge of the military forces (the Army, Navy, Air Force, and Marines). The Constitution was designed so that the president and Congress must share the responsibility of declaring war, but in case of emergency the president may declare war without congressional approval.

2. Chief Administrator

The president is in charge of appointing people to fill government jobs.

3. Chief Diplomat

The president is the country's representative to the rest of the world. The president can make treaties (with the Senate's approval), nominate diplomats (if the Senate approves), and host visitors from other countries.

4. Chief Legislator

The president is in charge of giving Congress a list of items that are important and timely. Congress must discuss and propose action for each of these items. If the president doesn't like the result of Congress' vote, he or she can vote against it by using a veto.

5. Chief Magistrate

The president is in charge of seeing that the laws of the United States are followed and obeyed.

HOW IS A PRESIDENT ELECTED?

Every four years, the United States chooses someone to be president and someone to be vice president. This election process is done in two steps: a primary election and a general election.

In the primary election, candidates for president compete for the nomination of his or her political party, such as the Democratic, Republican, and Libertarian parties. Each candidate gets committed delegates (which are like points) based on the number of votes they get in each state. The date of the primary election may be different from state to state. During the summer of an election year, each political party holds a convention and adds up the delegates for each person running for president. The candidate with over half the total delegates gets the nomination of his or her party. The winner then chooses someone to run as vice president on the "ticket."

In the general election, the winners of the primary election face off against each other. Sometimes independent candidates (people without a political party) join in the race too. The general election is always held in early November. When all the votes are added up at the end of election day, the candidate with the most votes in a state wins all the delegates (called electoral votes) in that state. (These delegates form what is called the electoral college.) The number of electoral votes for each state is equal to the number of the state's members in Congress—two senators plus the representatives. There are 535 total electoral votes in the 50 states. The candidate who gets 268 or more electoral votes wins the presidency! (Think about this: It is possible to win the electoral vote and the presidency but come in second in the total number of votes by citizens, called the "popular vote.")

TTommy awoke in a puddle of drool.
He had fallen asleep preparing for school.
He looked at their work, they broke into smiles—
history gave them the THE TUPPERMAN FILES.

TTommy burst out the door, he couldn't be late.
Today was the day of the giant debate.

Penelope chose to give her speech first.
She said, "I am the best and he is the worst!
I promise you **everything** under the sun.
I am the **one** that represents fun."

(On the other hand...)

Tommy's speech would've made Honest Abe proud.
He stood smart and tall as he talked to the crowd.
He spoke of the truth and responsible acts,
To vote with your brain and consider the facts.
He stuck out his chest and said,

"I'm no **slob**—I am the one who will do the best **job**!"

The votes were all counted with the greatest of care,
And the time had arrived to finally declare:

A winner.

Mrs. Snodgrass opened a very small note
That had written on it the results of the vote.
She read it aloud as the students sat frozen.
It was, yes indeed, Tommy they'd chosen.

57

Tommy was hit by a **fuzzy** sensation, as the crowd gave him a standing ovation.
He noticed, however, while hearing the cheers, that smoke poured out of Penelope's ears.
She started to slobber and her eyes turned dark red,
She yelled, "Tommy Tupperman,

I'll step on your head!"

Mrs. Snodgrass grabbed
Penelope by the scruff of the neck,
and told the young lady
she might want to check
her schedule for things
that might interfere . . .

. . . with the detention she'll have
for the rest of the **year.**

So...

If you happen to visit Rhino Grade School,
You might want to consider one very big rule:

Whenever you leave in the middle of class,
You better have with you an official hall pass,
Because any attempt to walk down the hall
Is watched by the tops, the best of them all—

and

★ Tommy **Tupperman's** ★

his name!

HALL PASS

HALL MONITOR

All secure in the hall!

Ray Nelson is a great big guy. (He's six feet four inches tall and weighs 245 pounds.) Most people look at Ray and think he should be a professional wrestler. Ray's favorite president is George Washington because he wore a wig and was still cool enough to be president. Ray spends most of his time hanging out in Portland, Oregon, with his wife, Theresa, his daughter, Alexandria, and pet bear, Butch. (He also has a dog named Molly, who is half Great Dane and half Shetland pony.)

Douglas Kelly is a very small man. He lives in a renovated Malibu Barbie playhouse in Ray's garage. He enjoys jazz, golf, and painting. Doug's favorite president is the guy on the twenty dollar bill. (This is the biggest bill Doug has ever seen. Otherwise we guess he would probably like the guy on the thousand dollar bill.) Doug spends most of his spare time with Victoria and his cat, Toonces.

Ben Adams is a simple man with simple needs. Give Ben heavy metal music, a comic book, and some animal crackers, and he is as content as can be. Ben sports long brown hair and tiny little round glasses. Ben's favorite president is Benjamin Franklin. (Good thing Ben didn't write the educational information for this book.) Ben lives with his wife, Michelle, their two dogs, Maxx and Lilly, and 189 cats in Beaverton, Oregon.

Mike McLane used to have a successful career as a lawyer. Mike got tired of respect, a high salary, and job security, so he took a job with Flying Rhinoceros, Inc. Mike's favorite president is William Taft. Mike thinks a president should have sturdy thighs and a hardy appetite—traits for which Taft was notable. Mike lives in Portland, Oregon, with his wife, Holly, and their son, Benjamin.

HISTORICAL CONSULTANTS

Keith Melder is *curator emeritus* at the National Museum of American History, Smithsonian Institution. Keith is the author of *Hail to the Candidate*, a book about presidential elections.

M.W. Pete Smith has been a history teacher for 40 years. He is an expert on U.S. presidents and a collector of presidential campaign buttons.

SPECIAL THANKS

President Gerald Ford, Penny Circle, Bill and Vicky Meyer, Jim Wilson, Deborah Bielman, Jerry Sayer, Keith Gaumont, Theresa Nelson, Victoria Collins, Michelle Adams, Julie Mohr, Chris Nelson, Jen Jacobson, Kelly Kuntz, Joseph Siegel, and Janet Lockwood.